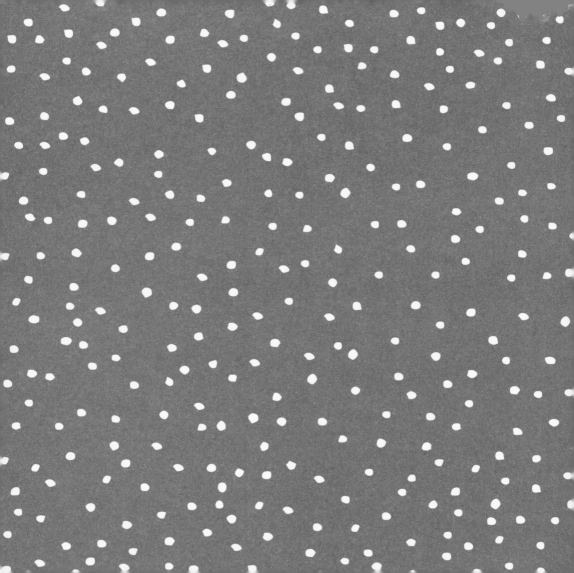

WEAR GRATITUDE
(LIKE A SWEATER)

ART + WORDS

to INSPIRE

ILLUSTRATIONS and HAND-LETTERING
BY SUSA TALAN

ROCK
POINT
ROCKPOINTPUB.COM
NEW YORK, NY

A division of Quarto Publishing Group USA Inc.
276 Fifth Avenue, Suite 206
New York, New York 10001

ROCK POINT and the distinctive Rock Point logo are trademarks of
Quarto Publishing Group USA Inc.

ISBN-13: 978-1-63106-028-1

Printed in China

2 4 6 8 10 9 7 5 3 1

www.rockpointpub.com

For my TEACHERS, with DEEPeSt GratituDE.

For ALEXiS, My LOVE and BEST FriEND.

and

For THEO, ALexandeR and NiCO:

"THErE iS NO REMEdY FoR LOVE,
BUt to LOVE MORE."

-HENRY DAViD THOreau

❧ Introduction ❧

Growing up in New England, I've always worn sweaters: hand-knitted, wool or acrylic, turtleneck, V-neck, button-down, country wrap, or city sleek. I love sweaters. And that's a good thing, because it's impossible to make it through a proper New England winter—or any cold night for that matter—without them.

So what does it mean to *wear gratitude like a sweater?* It means taking comfort in a daily practice that holds what I value close by, like a warm layer or second skin. If I *wear* gratitude, it means that I carry it with me, and I'm surrounded by an outlook that says, *There are so many reasons to be grateful and to notice the good*. Sometimes it takes effort to find what I'm grateful for, especially with all the ways that life can tug and overwhelm, or in the face of real hardship. But that's what interests me about gratitude; it's a practice that's useful in real life.

The drawings in this book came about as a result of a year-long challenge to work with Art + Words to create a daily representation of the things I was grateful for, especially as they arose in my daily life. I'd gone to art school many years before, but something about that experience had made me suspicious—my paintings were technical and sterile, and I'd been yearning for a way back to my art.

Two years ago, I was living in rural Massachusetts in a studio surrounded by two hundred acres and a lot of quiet. I'd spent the previous five years developing a meditation practice, which I sought out after a family crisis shook me up and brought what mattered into focus. I put questions about art and my career on hold and immersed myself in mindfulness and meditation. I watered plants and hung laundry. I became interested in my mind and discovered what kinds of thoughts and attitudes led me to feel a sense of ease or confusion. I discovered the value of listening. Perhaps most significantly, I came to appreciate the importance of wisdom—the kind of wisdom that you read about in books or find in teachers or wise friends, as well as the kind of wisdom that bubbles up from within. This led me to greater awareness, to learning deeper forms of generosity, compassion, and, yes, to gratitude. It is a practice that both changed and, in many ways, saved my life—from the inside out.

While living in the middle of a December forest, I was preparing to turn forty. Life moves fast—a blink on the cosmic scene. It was time to let my quiet creative dream live or die. I could feel it: Now or never, girl. One moment, I was looking out the window. And the next, I was drawing eggs, lots of them—birth, newness, celebration. And then I was posting on my brand new blog, 365 Days of Gratitude. Day 1: All you good eggs out there. And you difficult ones, too. I began as an egg. What am I now? Grateful. And with that, it began. Drawings. Gratitude.

Not surprisingly, my relationship to gratitude evolved over the course of the project. In the beginning, I was so focused on getting a piece of work out every day that I had to remind myself what I was grateful for. That sounds funny, but it really feels like part of the path of being human. Don't we all need reminders to be kind, to feel something directly and not just think about it? I have found this to be true in my relationship to most meaningful practices. They require a kind of effort and return. Over and over again. To listen, to observe, to be kind, to come back to the present moment.

Gratitude is still something I have to actively cultivate, but now it's a kind of companion. My mind has more capacity to stay with what is precious and to meet challenges with deeper resilience. You could say that I wear gratitude now, like a familiar garment, and I am happiest when I take it with me wherever I go.

I hope this book and the practice of gratitude will be a friend to you on the path; a welcome resource that's both mobile and meaningful; a pause in the big pond of daily life. Use it to inspire gratitude or simply to recall what matters most—in this moment and the next.

This BEING
human
is A GUEST house.
EVERY MORNING
A NEW
ARRiVAL.

– Rumi

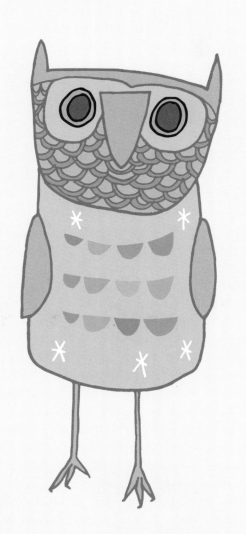

KNOWING
YOURSELF
is the
BEGINNING
OF ALL
WISDOM.

- Aristotle

THERE IS SOME thing in every ONE of you THAT WAITS and LISTENS for the SOUND of the GENUINE in yourSELF.

- HOWARD THURMAN

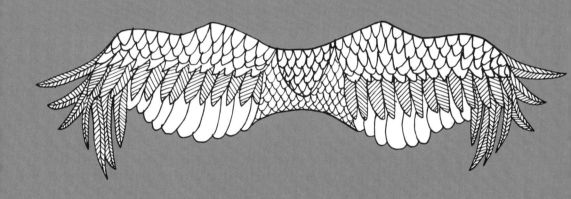

SOMEthing OPENS

OuR WINGS.

- Rumi

THE WHOLE WORLD IS A SERIES OF MIRACLES, BUT WE'RE SO USED TO THEM WE CALL them ORDINARY THINGS.

—HANS CHRISTIAN ANDERSEN

The SEA IS A CONTINUAL MIRACLE.

- WALT WHITMAN

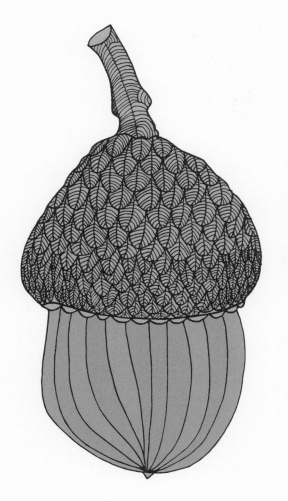

THE
CREATION
OF A
THOUSAND
FORESTS
is in
ONE
ACORN

- EMERSON

WHAT LiES
BEHiND us
and WHAT
LiES BEFORE us
are tiny Matters
COMPARED to
WHAT LiES
within us.

- RALPH WALDO EMERSON

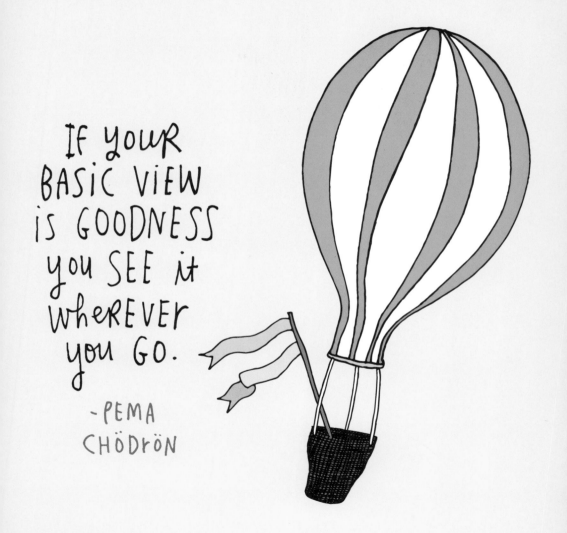

IF YOUR
BASIC VIEW
IS GOODNESS
YOU SEE it
WHEREVER
YOU GO.

-PEMA
CHÖDRÖN

you BECOME WHAT
you think ABOUT
ALL DAY LONG.

- RALPH WALDO EMERSON

MY RELIGION IS KINDNESS.
- DALAI LAMA

ME, We.

—MUHAMMED ALi

Everything CONNECTS to everything ELSE.

—Leonardo Da Vinci

A thousand fibers connect us.

– HERMAN MELVILLE

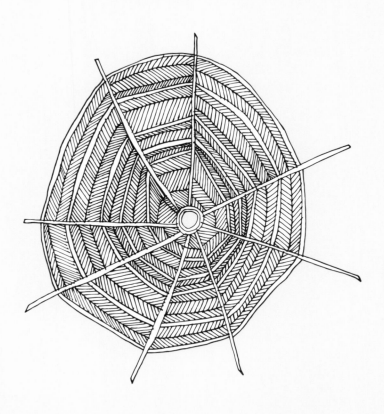

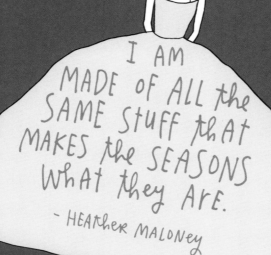

I AM
MADE OF ALL the
SAME stuff that
MAKES the SEASONS
what they are.

- HEATHER MALONEY

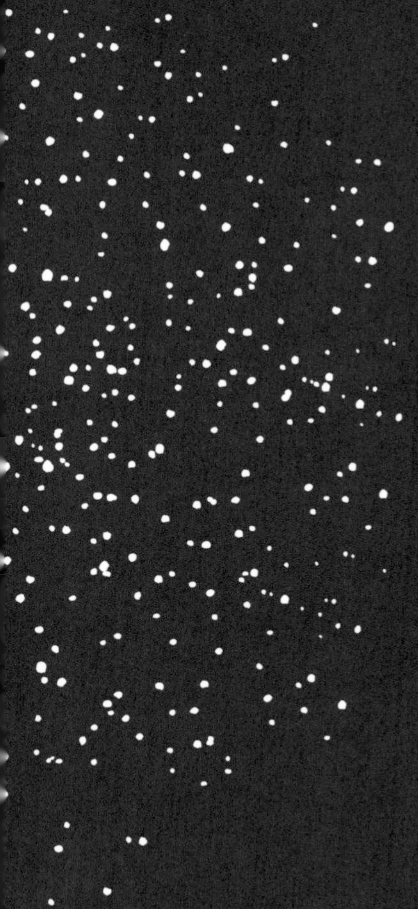

A LEAF of GRASS
is NO LESS than
the JOURNEY-WORK
of the STARS.

- WALT WHITMAN

EVERYTHING CHANGES.

I AM
MADE and
REMADE
CONTINUALLY.
-Virginia WOOLF

NOTHING is LOST,
EVERYTHING is TRANSFORMED.

-ANTOINE LAVOISIER

I WILL BiND WHAT
NATURE SCATTERS
I WiLL WEAVE WiTh
WHAT I'VE GAThERED

- HEAThER MALONEY

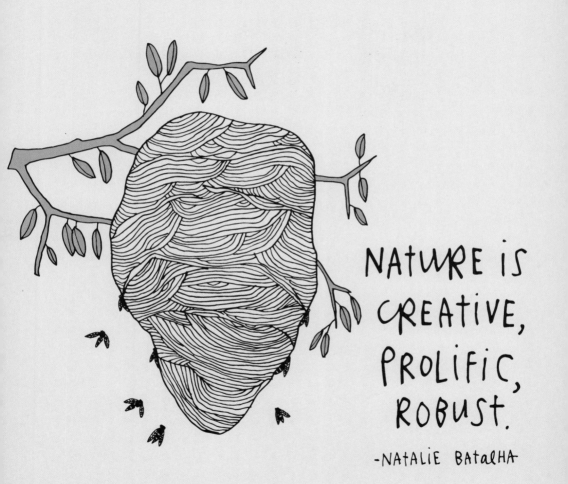

NATURE IS CREATIVE, PROLIFIC, ROBUST.

-NATALIE BATALHA

IN EACH OF US, there IS
A little VOICE that KNOWS
EXActly WHICH WAY to GO.

-ALICE WALKER

SO MANY WAYS to TRAVEL
At the PACE of OBSERVATION.

PAY ATTENTION to the INTRICATE PATTERNS of YOUR EXISTENCE.

-DOUG DILLON

I AM
DETERMINED
to PRACTICE
DEEP Listening.
-THICH Nhat Hanh

KEEP OBSErViNG UNTiL
THiNGS UNFOLD NatuRALLY.

-SAYADaw U TEJANiYA

it's NOT WHAT you LOOK AT that MATTERS, it's WHAT you SEE.

—HENRY DAVID THOREAU

WIPE the DEW off
your SPECTACLES
AND See that the
WORLD is MOVING.

- ELIZABETH CADY STANTON

ONLY that
DAY DAWNS
to which
WE ARE
AWAKE.

- HENRY DAVID THOREAU

the SLOW overcomes the FAST.

−LAO TZU

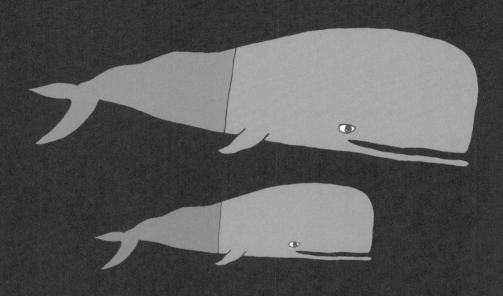

JUST KEEP GOING
NO FEELING is FINAL.

- RAINER MARIA RILKE

AND the DAY CAME when the RISK to REMAIN TIGHT in A BUD WAS MORE Painful thAN the RISK it TOOK to BLOSSOM.

— anonymous

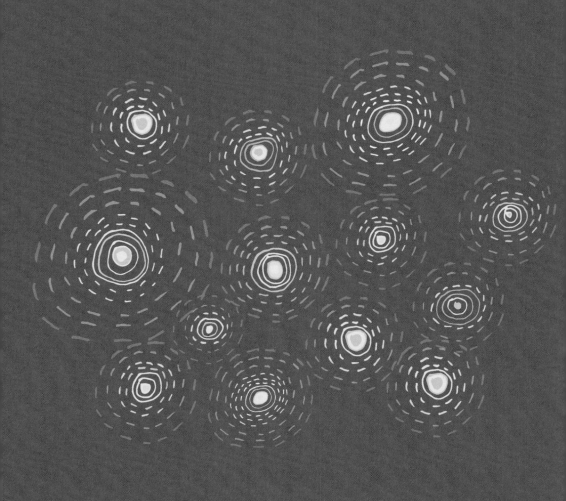

the DARKER the NIGHT,
THE BRIGHTER the STARS.
-FYODOR DOSTOYEVSKY

SUCCESS is sometimes
the OUTCOME of A WHOLE
String of FAILURES.
- VINCENT van GOGH

TURN YOURSELF AROUND.

-HEATHER MALONEY

BLOOM
where
you
ARE
PLANTED.
— Saint FRANCIS de SALES

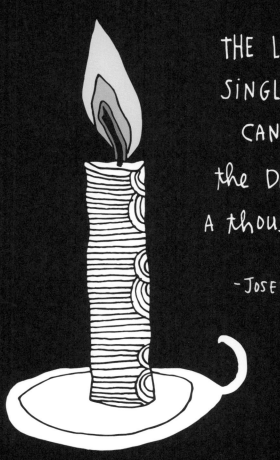

THE LIGHT of A
SINGLE CANDLE
CAN DISPEL
the DARKNESS of
A thousAND YEARS.

–JOSEPH GOLDSTEIN

LET US KEEP COURAGE
AND try to BE
PATIENT and GENTLE.

-VINCENT van VOGH

EVERY WALL IS A DOOR.

- RALPH WALDO EMERSON

LOOK
INWARD.
DON'T LET
the true
NATURE of
ANYTHING
elude you.

-MARCUS AURELIUS

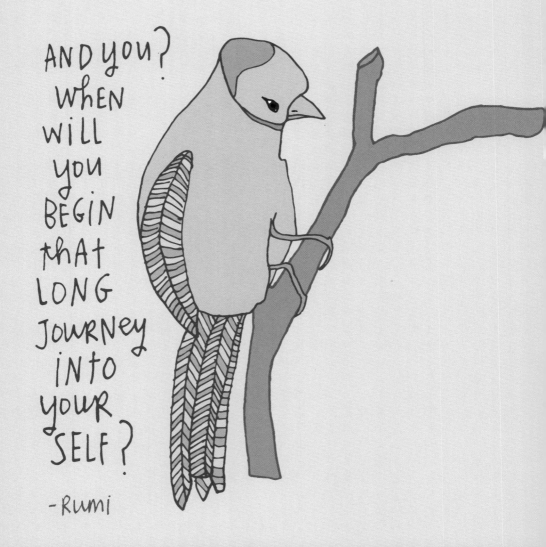

AND you?
WHEN
WiLL
you
BEGIN
tHAt
LONG
JOuRNey
iNTO
youR
SELF?

-Rumi

the MORE I KNOW MYSELF,
THE more I LISTen.

-HOLLY WREN SPAULDING

I AM DETERMINED to PRACTICE LOVING SPEECH.

-THICH Nhat Hanh

to A
MIND
that
is
still
the
whole
universe
surrenders.

- LAO Tzu

EQUANIMITY IS
SEEING the
WORLD with
SOFT EYES.

-KAMALA MASTERS

BE SILLY.

BE HONEST.

BE KIND.

-RALPH WALDO EMERSON

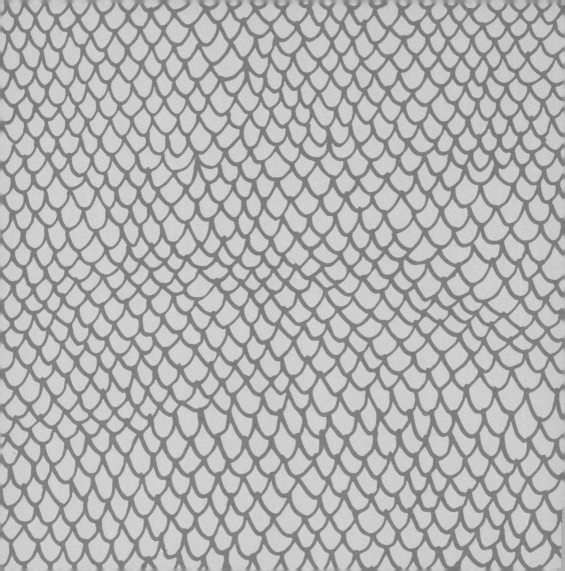

BE A PATTERN for the WORLD.
—LAO TZU

RE-EXAMINE all you
HAVE BEEN told.

—WALT WHITMAN

WE DON'T HAVE
to TAKE the
STORY AS truth.

—JACK KORNFIELD

HAPPINESS
is the
ABSENCE
of the STRIVING
for HAPPINESS.
- CHuang-tzu

WHEN WE
RELEASE that
STRIVING FOR
SOMEWHERE and
SOMETHING ELSE,
WE COME HOME.

- KAREN MAEZEN MILLER

PEACE
COMES
FROM
WITHIN.

- BuddHA

WHERE
WORDS
FAIL,
MUSIC
SPEAKS.
- HANS CHRISTIAN
ANDERSEN

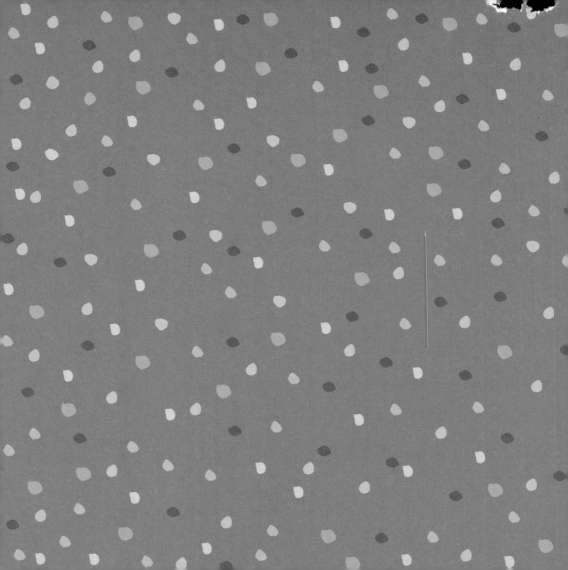

I FIND it WHOLESOME
to BE ALONE.

-HenRy DAViD THOReau

LOVE
YOUR
SOLITUDE.

- RAINER MARIA
RILKE

LOVE
PEOPLE.

(HOLD them in YOUR HEART).

LOVE IN SUCH A WAY that the PERSON you LOVE feels FREE.

-THICH Nhat Hanh

WE WEre
together.
I FORGEt
the REST.

- WALT WhitMAN

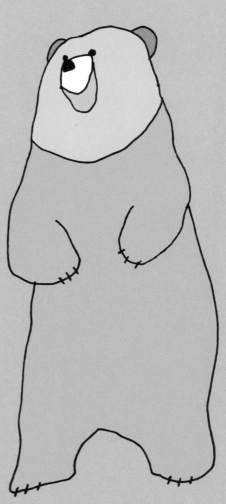

THIS UNIVERSE
is MUCH TOO BIG
to HOLD ONto,
But it iS
tHE PERFECT
SiZE FOR
LEttiNG GO.

-SHARON SALZBERG

Life is a Journey, Not a Destination.

- RALPH WALDO EMERSON

LIFE IS FRAGILE
and SHORT
AND WORTH ALL the
LOVING PRESENCE
WE CAN bring
to it.

-REBECCA KUSHINS

WALK as if you
are KISSING the
EARTH with YOUR FEET.

−THICH NHAT HANH

WALK BESIDE ME and BE MY FRIEND.

-ANONYMOUS

WE CAN DO
small things
with GREAT LOVE.

-MOTHER TERESA

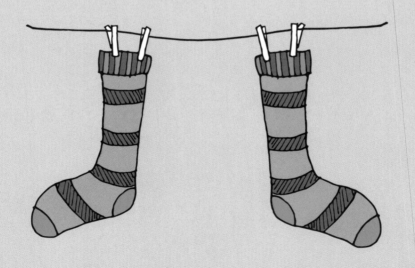

THE BEST WAY to KNOW LiFE is to LOVE MANY things.

-vincent van GOGH

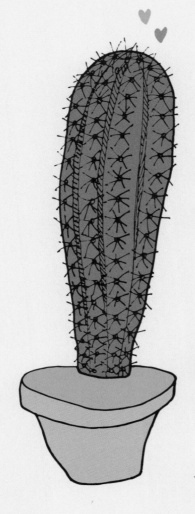

THERE
IS NO
CHARM
EQUAL
to the
TENDERNESS
of HEART.

-JANE AUSTEN

EACH MOMENT
IS A CHANCE
for US to
MAKE PEACE
with THE
WORLD.

-THICH NhAt HANh

This being human is a guest house. Every morning a new arrival." "Something opens our wings." "And you? When will you begin that long journey into yourself." **—Rumi, translated by Coleman Barks. All quotes are copyright © Coleman Barks, used by permission of translator.**

"I am made of all the same stuff that makes the seasons what they are." "I will weave what nature scatters, I will bind with what I've gathered." "Turn yourself around."**—Heather Maloney. Used by permission of author.**

"I am made and remade continually."**—Virginia Woolf. Permission granted: The Society of Authors as the Literary Representative of the Estate of Virginia Woolf.**

"Nature is creative, prolific, robust." **—Natalie Batalha. Used by permission of author**.

"In each of us, there is a little voice that knows exactly which way to go."**—Alice Walker. Used by permission of author.**

"Pay attention to the intricate patterns of your existence [that you take for granted]."**—Doug Dillon. Copyright © Doug Dillon. Used by permission of author.**

"I am determined to practice deep listening." I am determined to practice loving speech" "[You must] Love in such a way that the person you love feels free." "Walk as if you are kissing the Earth with your feet." "Each moment is a chance for us to make peace with the world."**—Thich Nhat Hanh. All quotes are copyright © Parallax Press and used by permission. www.parallax.org**

"[Just acknowledge, accept, and] Keep observing until things unfold naturally." **—Sayadaw U Tejaniya. Used by permission of author.**

"[Just as] The light of a single candle can dispel the darkness of a thousand years."**—Joseph Goldstein. From *A HEART FULL OF PEACE* © 2007. Reprinted by arrangement with Wisdom Publication.**

"We don't have to take the story as truth."**—Jack Kornfield. From *THE WISE HEART* by Jack Kornfield © 2009. Used by permission of author.**

"When we release that striving for somewhere and something else, we come home."**—Karen Maezen Miller. Used by permission of author.**

"Love People, hold them in your heart." "So many ways to travel at the pace of observation."**—Susa Talan, copyright © Susa Talan.**

"This universe is much too big to hold onto, but it is the perfect size for letting go."**—Sharon Salzberg. From *LOVINGKINDNESS* by Sharon Salzberg © 1995. Reprinted by arrangement with Shambhala Publications, Inc. www.shambhala.com**

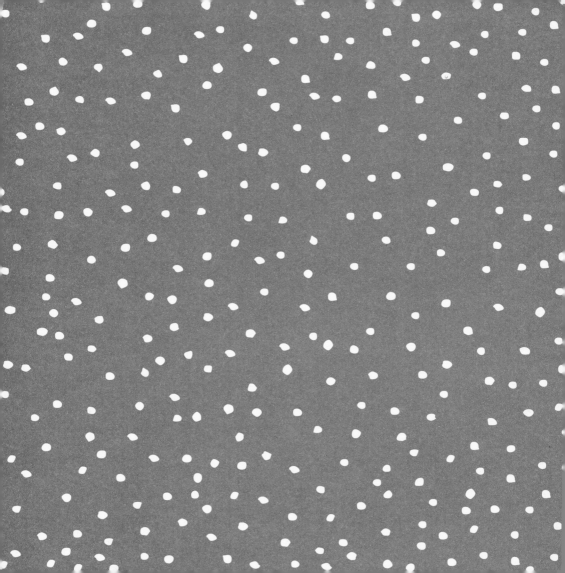

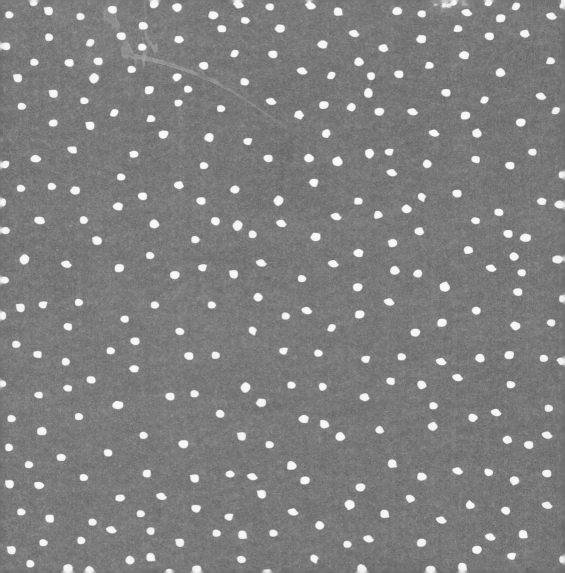